W9-CJZ-893

Steve Irwin

Heidi Moore

Chicago, Illinois

J BIOG
IRWIN

HEINEMANN-RAINTREE

TO ORDER:
☎ Phone Customer Service **888-454-2279**
💻 Visit **www.heinemannraintree.com** to browse our catalog and order online.

©2009 Raintree
a division of Pearson Inc.
Chicago, Illinois

Editorial: Louise Galpine, Rachel Howells, and Adam Miller
Design: Kimberly R. Miracle and Betsy Wernert
Illustrations: Mapping Specialists, Inc.
Picture Research: Mica Brancic and Helen O'Reilly
Production: Vicki Fitzgerald

Originated by Modern Age
Printed and bound in China by Leo Paper Group.

ISBN-13: 978-1-4109-3223-5 (hc)
ISBN-10: 1-4109-3223-0 (hc)

13 12 11 10
10 9 8 7 6 5 4 3 2

Library of Congress Cataloging-in-Publication Data
Moore, Heidi, 1976-
  Steve Irwin / Heidi Moore.
    p. cm. -- (Great naturalists)
  Includes bibliographical references and index.
  ISBN 978-1-4109-3223-5 (hc)
  1. Irwin, Steve--Juvenile literature. 2. Herpetologists--Australia--Biography--Juvenile literature. 3. Naturalists--Australia--Biography--Juvenile literature. I. Title.
  QL31.I78M66 2008
  597.9092--dc22
  [B]
                    2007049814

Acknowledgments
The author and publishers are grateful to the following for permission to reproduce copyright material: © Camera Press pp. **5**, **18** (Fotoblitz/Stills/Gamma); © Corbis pp. **15** (Tobias Bernhard/Zefa), **19** (Australia Zoo/Handout/Reuters), **21** (Najlah Feanny), **22** (Reuters), **23** (Jamie Fawcett/epa), **24** (Vera Devai/epa), **25** (Tony Phillips/epa), **27** (Dave Hunt/epa); © Fotolia/Cedric Chabal) p. **11**; © istockphoto p. **13** (Neil Sullivan); © National Portrait Gallery p. **26** (Robin Sellick); © Nature Picture Library pp. **17 top** (Richard Du Toit), **17 bottom** (Steven David Miller); © Newspix/News Ltd. pp. **7-10**, **12** (Courier Mail).

Cover photograph of Steve Irwin reproduced with permission of ©Getty Images (Justin Sullivan).

The publishers would like to thank Nancy Harris for her assistance in the preparation of this book.

CONTENTS

Some words are shown in bold, **like this**. You can find out what they mean by looking in the glossary.

CROCODILE HUNTER

Millions of fans called him the **Crocodile** Hunter. But Steve Irwin did not hunt crocodiles for food or for sport. He trapped crocodiles to keep them safe from harm. And he had lots of fun doing it!

Irwin loved all animals, but most of all crocodiles. He called them "crocs" for short. Irwin was hooked on crocs from the time he was a child. The fierce animals amazed him.

All his life, Irwin loved nature. He became a **naturalist**. He believed it was important to study and respect nature. He was also a **conservationist**. He felt it was important to protect wildlife.

Croc teacher

As an adult, Irwin taught many people about crocs. He wanted people to see the animals as he did. He loved crocodiles. He did not see them as scary creatures.

What is a croc?

A crocodile is a type of **reptile**. Crocodiles feed on fish and other reptiles. They sometimes feed on large **mammals** such as zebra and wildebeest. They are one of nature's deadliest **predators**.

Irwin showed off his favorite animals in live wildlife shows. Then he showed them off on television and in movies. Irwin was friendly and outgoing. He gained fans around the world. Because of Steve Irwin, people all over the world are now hooked on crocs, too!

Irwin got closer than most people would to a crocodile! His extreme tricks shocked and delighted people all over the world.

A WILD CHILDHOOD

February 22, 1962, was a special day. Lyn and Bob Irwin were excited. Lyn was about to give birth. She had a baby boy! They named him Stephen Robert. Everyone called him Steve.

The Irwins lived in a big city—Melbourne, Australia. Australia is a large country with lots of interesting wildlife.

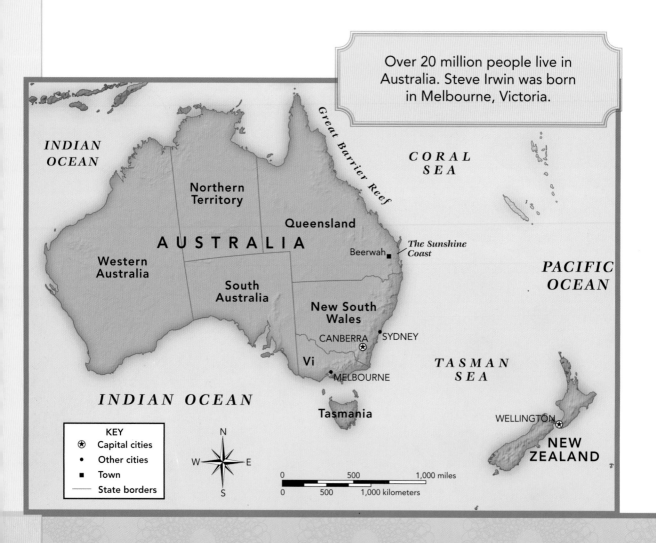

Over 20 million people live in Australia. Steve Irwin was born in Melbourne, Victoria.

INDIAN OCEAN

Northern Territory

Great Barrier Reef

CORAL SEA

Queensland

AUSTRALIA

Western Australia

Beerwah

The Sunshine Coast

PACIFIC OCEAN

South Australia

New South Wales

CANBERRA

SYDNEY

Vi

MELBOURNE

TASMAN SEA

INDIAN OCEAN

Tasmania

WELLINGTON

NEW ZEALAND

KEY
⊛ Capital cities
• Other cities
■ Town
— State borders

N
W   E
S

0   500   1,000 miles
0   500   1,000 kilometers

Steve is at the right of this photograph, dressed in black and white. It was the eighth birthday of his friend Mal.

Move to Queensland

Steve turned eight years old in 1970. That year the Irwins moved to Queensland. This is a large state in Australia. Queensland is home to the largest number of different kinds of animals in the country.

The Irwins settled on the sunny east coast. It is called the Sunshine Coast. It lies along the Pacific Ocean. Bob and Lyn Irwin planned to open a **reptile** and **fauna** park there. The park would be like a very small zoo. It would take in rescued (saved) reptiles, such as **crocodiles,** and other animals (fauna), such as kangaroos.

A birthday surprise

Steve Irwin's parents gave him a pet for his sixth birthday. It was a scrub python (a type of snake). Steve named him Fred. Fred the python was 12 feet (3.7 meters) long! Steve caught fish and mice to feed to him.

The Irwins worked hard at building Beerwah. Here Bob Irwin puts the finishing touches to this crocodile display, which was carved out of the wood of a 100-year-old tree.

Building Beerwah

Lyn and Bob Irwin worked on building the zoo. They called it Beerwah **Reptile** and **Fauna** Park. They lived in a trailer in the park. Steve and his two sisters lived there, too.

Steve's father was a **herpetologist**. A herpetologist studies reptiles. His mother was a wildlife caretaker. She helped to rescue **crocodiles**, poisonous snakes, and many other animals.

Animal friends

Often the Irwins released animals back into the wild. But some animals were too sick or hurt to live in the wild. Others would have been in danger from humans or other animals. Steve's family brought these animals to Beerwah.

Many children grow up with pets such as dogs or goldfish. Steve and his sisters grew up around kangaroos and koalas!

Steve says
"What a childhood!" Steve later remembered. "It was nothing for us kids to be sharing our house with **orphaned** joey [baby] kangaroos, … koala joeys, baby birds, and … other injured Australian animals."

Steve learned a lot about animals from his parents. He learned not to fear animals that many people find scary. He also learned to handle deadly animals such as poisonous snakes.

There weren't many animals that Irwin was scared of! Here he is with a python in 1987. Pythons squeeze their prey to death.

Blocks of crocs

One of Steve Irwin's favorite animals was the **crocodile**. But in the 1970s Australian crocs were in danger. People were hunting them. The crocodile was losing its **habitat** (home). The Irwins worried it might become **extinct**. Then there would be no more crocodiles.

So Bob Irwin learned how to trap crocs. Some he released into a safer area in the wild. Others he brought to live at Beerwah. Over time the Irwins took in dozens of crocodiles.

This family photograph shows a young Irwin handling a baby crocodile.

It is important to breed new creatures in zoos, such as this baby croc.

A bigger Beerwah

For years Beerwah **Reptile** and **Fauna** Park grew and grew. In 1980 the Irwins bought more land to make the park bigger. This gave the crocodiles and other animals more space to roam. They changed the name to Queensland Reptile and Fauna Park. Soon the crocs at the park started **breeding**. Breeding produces new creatures.

Jumping crocs

Steve's father taught him how to jump crocs. First, they would track a river crocodile. Then, they wrestled and trapped the croc. Finally, they tied it with rope. This way it could not get loose. Steve jumped his first croc when he was just nine years old. It was 3 feet (91 centimeters) long. Please do not try this at home!

12

CATCH AND RELEASE

Steve and Alister the **Alligator** pose for the camera.

Steve Irwin finished high school in 1979. Then he struck out on his own. He took a job with the Queensland Parks and Wildlife Service. This is a group that saves wildlife and protects nature.

Irwin's job was to rescue **crocodiles**. Some of the crocs lived too close to people. Others were a danger to pets or farm animals. It was hot, hard work. Irwin chased crocs through creeks, rivers, and swamps. He wrestled the fierce animals in the mud. It took skill to catch one. Then he would release it in a safer area away from people.

Endangered crocs

Many crocodiles were in danger from **poachers**. Poachers are people who hunt illegally. Australia made crocodile hunting against the law in 1974. But that did not stop many people from hunting them. Some poachers hunted crocs for sport. Others wanted the crocodiles' skin. Some people want shoes or handbags made out of scaly crocodile skin!

Work for free?

The Queensland Parks and Wildlife Service did not pay Irwin for his work. He was a **volunteer**. That means he worked for free. He did this because he really wanted to help save crocs.

A purse that looks like this could be made out of crocodile skin.

Croc park

Sometimes Irwin could not find a good place in the wild for his rescued **crocodiles**. Then he would bring them to his family's **reptile** park.

Irwin and his father designed their own crocodile trap. They made it out of soft mesh. It was like a spiderweb made of rope. Some fishermen use the same type of trap to catch fish.

Waiting to trap

Bob and Steve Irwin would place the trap at the water's edge. They would wait for a crocodile to climb in and grab the bait. Then, snap! The trap's opening pulls shut. The croc cannot get out. The soft mesh does not hurt the animals. But it is very good at trapping them.

Steve Irwin was very good at catching crocs. He and his dad decided to build a special crocodile park on their land. They built the park in 1987. This gave the crocs a larger **habitat**. Now the Irwins could save even more crocodiles from **poachers**!

Croc fact

Crocodiles speed through water and over land. They can swim up to 20 miles (32 kilometers) per hour. On land they can run up to 11 miles (18 kilometers) per hour.

Crocodile handler

Irwin's adventures heated up in the late 1980s. He got very skilled at **crocodile** trapping. He moved dozens of crocodiles to safety.

Irwin often went home to his family's **reptile** and **fauna** park. There he showed off his crocodile handling skills. He led croc **demonstrations**, or shows, for park visitors. People watched from behind a fence.

Irwin threw chunks of food toward a waiting crocodile. The huge croc would catch the tasty treat with a swift snap of its powerful jaws. The crowd would gasp and then clap with delight.

By 1990 people came from all over Australia to see Irwin's amazing crocodile shows.

Croc or gator?

Crocodiles and **alligators** (gators) look alike. They are both scaly reptiles. They have long bodies and short legs. How can you tell them apart?

Alligators have wider, rounded snouts. Crocodiles' snouts are thin and pointed. With its mouth closed, a crocodile shows the fourth tooth on its lower jaw. But there are many types of gators and crocs. Ask a wildlife expert if you want to know for sure!

A crocodile, above, shows its fourth bottom tooth. An alligator, below, has a wide, rounded snout.

FINDING A MATE

Steve Irwin was not just skilled with **crocodiles**. He also handled other animals, such as snakes and giant tortoises. Irwin loved to thrill park visitors. He showed off all kinds of creatures. He would hold up an animal and say, "Isn't he gorgeous?"

Irwin's animal demos wowed visitors to the Queensland **Reptile** and **Fauna** Park. One of these visitors was an American woman. Her name was Terri Raines. Raines was on a trip to Australia in 1991. She visited the park and took in a croc demo. She loved watching Irwin handle the fierce creatures. She wanted to meet him, so she did!

Terri Raines and Steve Irwin married on June 4, 1992. Soon Terri was feeding crocs along with Steve!

After meeting Steve Irwin, Terri came to love crocs, too.

Terri and Steve Irwin pose at their zoo with Harriet, a Galapagos giant land tortoise. Nobody knows exactly how old she was when she died, but she was thought to be 176 years old!

Meet Terri Irwin

Terri Raines was born on July 20, 1964. She grew up in the state of Oregon. Her family taught her about **conservation**. She believed in caring for wildlife. Terri ran her own wildlife rescue center called Cougar Country in the United States. After marrying Irwin, she went to live in Australia. She became Irwin's partner and fellow wildlife caretaker.

CROCODILE HUNTER ON TV

Steve and Terri Irwin took over Queensland **Reptile** and **Fauna** Park. By then the park was very popular. Many people came to see the **rare** animals. They stayed to watch the wild **crocodile** demonstrations. In 1992 Steve and Terri Irwin made the park even bigger. They gave it a new name—Australia Zoo.

Later that year, Irwin got a phone call. It was his friend John Stainton. Stainton worked in television. Stainton had a question for Irwin. Stainton asked if he could make a video of Irwin trapping crocodiles. He wanted to put the show on TV.

That wildlife show became *The Crocodile Hunter*. Australian television aired the show in 1992. That program launched the Irwins onto TV and changed their lives forever!

Caught on camera

Irwin's father gave him a video camera in the 1980s. He filmed himself catching crocs in northern Queensland. Stainton got his hands on these home movies. The movies gave him the idea for the TV show. He knew people would be amazed to see the "Crocodile Hunter" in action.

People came to Australia Zoo to see **alligators**, as well as crocs.

Irwin's show was a high-energy performance. In this photograph he holds a rattlesnake!

Now showing—everywhere!

Soon The **Crocodile** Hunter was showing all over the world. It aired in the United States, Great Britain, and many other countries. Both children and adults enjoyed watching the show. Viewers fell in love with Steve Irwin. He was a daring wildlife handler. He thrilled viewers with deadly crocs, snakes, and spiders.

Steve Irwin went to the opening of *The Crocodile Hunter* with Terri and Bindi Sue.

Crikey!

Irwin loved to show off his favorite creatures. And he did it in his own special way. Irwin became famous for his sayings, such as "Crocs rule!" and "Crikey!" ("Crikey" is a word that shows surprise, like "Wow!") Viewers never knew what Irwin would do or say next. But it was almost always wild and exciting.

Irwin went home to his Australia Zoo all the time. He still led wildlife shows there. In person, the friendly Australian seemed just like he was on TV!

A growing family

Steve and Terri Irwin had two children. On July 24, 1998, they had a baby girl. They named her Bindi Sue. Robert Clarence, known as Bob, was born on December 1, 2003. Both are taking after their parents. They are learning to be wildlife caretakers.

Irwin lures a croc out of its pond at Australia Zoo with a tasty treat.

Australia Zoo

Today, people come from all over to visit Australia Zoo. They want to see the **Crocodile** Hunter's famous creatures up close!

Australia Zoo has won many awards. It is known for its great **exhibits** and wildlife rescues. Big cats prowl the zoo's Tiger Temple display. Falcons and eagles glide through the air in the Birds of Prey house. The zoo is also thought to have the world's largest **wombat** area. A wombat is a small **mammal** with claws and sharp teeth.

The zoo's biggest draw is the Crocoseum. This is a huge dome with clear ponds. Here the crocs swim, feed, and show off with their handlers.

Salties and freshies

Two types of crocodiles live in Australia. One is the saltwater croc, or saltie. The other is the freshwater croc, or freshie. Salties have a wider snout. They also grow much larger than freshies. You can see both types of crocs at Australia Zoo.

Big cats could also be found at Australia Zoo. This tiger cub (baby) is six weeks old.

Movie star

Irwin went on to star in other programs. Millions tuned in to watch his shows on the TV channel Animal Planet. They were called *The Crocodile Hunter's Croc Files* and *The Crocodile Hunter Diaries*. Then Irwin made a movie. *Crocodile Hunter: Collision Course* came out in 2002. It starred Steve Irwin!

WILDLIFE WARRIORS

Steve and Terri Irwin never stopped saving animals. They founded the International **Crocodile** Rescue group around 2002. The group rescues crocs around the world.

In 2002 they started Wildlife Warriors Worldwide. It aims to protect injured or **endangered** wildlife. Endangered animals are in danger of dying out.

Steve Irwin would have gone on to save many more animals. He would have starred in more TV shows and movies. But something awful happened in 2006. Irwin was filming a show near Australia's Great Barrier Reef. Many fish and sea creatures live in this part of the ocean. The show was called *The Ocean's Deadliest*.

Irwin rescued many animals, including elephants.

Thousands of fans left flowers in memory of the "Crocodile Hunter."

A terrible accident

One day Irwin went swimming in the water. Suddenly he came across a **stingray**. Its sharp **barb** (stinger) came up and stabbed his chest. Irwin died on September 4, 2006. He was only 44 years old.

Fans around the world were upset. But Irwin died doing what he loved best. Some people thought he took too many risks. But millions loved him. For years he thrilled viewers with his daring moves. He also taught people the need for **conservation**, or saving animals. "Crocodile Hunter" Steve Irwin showed the world that "Crocs rule!"

TIMELINES

Steve Irwin's life

1962	Born on February 22.
1970	Irwins move to Queensland, Australia.
	Beerwah **Reptile** and **Fauna** Park opens.
1971	Steve Irwin jumps his first **crocodile**.
1979	Irwin finishes high school.
1980	Beerwah is made larger; it becomes Queensland Reptile and Fauna Park.
1980s	Irwin traps crocs in northern Queensland swamps.
1990s	Queensland Reptile and Fauna Park draws lots of visitors.
1992	Steve Irwin marries American Terri Raines on June 4.
	The Crocodile Hunter airs on Australian TV.
1992–PRESENT	*The Crocodile Hunter* appears on TV in the United States, Great Britain, and all over the world.
1998	Bindi Sue Irwin is born on July 24.
2001	Irwin appears in movie *Doctor Doolittle 2*.
2002	Irwin appears in movie *Crocodile Hunter: Collision Course*.
	Steve and Terri Irwin found Wildlife Warriors Worldwide.
2003	Robert Clarence (Bob) Irwin is born on December 1.
2004	Steve and Terri Irwin found Australian Wildlife Hospital.
2006	Steve Irwin dies on September 4. He was swimming and was stabbed by a **stingray**.

World timeline

1888 National Geographic Society founded in Washington, DC.

1961 World Wildlife Fund founded to protect **endangered** species and their **habitats**.

1962 *Silent Spring* by U.S. writer Rachel Carson is published; it sparks environmental movement.

1966 U.S. **naturalist** Dian Fossey begins study of mountain gorillas.

1971 Greenpeace is founded to protect the environment.

1974 Australia makes crocodile hunting illegal.

1996 Cable TV channel Animal Planet launches.

LATE 1990s Millions tune in to watch *The Crocodile Hunter's Croc Files* and *The Crocodile Hunter Diaries* on Animal Planet.

2006 Al Gore's movie *An Inconvenient Truth* brings attention to the **global warming** crisis.

  November 15 is declared Steve Irwin Day.

2007 American crocodile is removed from endangered species list.

GLOSSARY

alligator thick-skinned reptile that lives in the water and has a broad snout. Many alligators live in southern Florida.

barb stinger. A scorpion strikes its prey with its sharp barb.

breeding mating to produce new creatures. Zoo owners want to make sure that their animals keep breeding.

conservation protecting something, such as a natural resource

conservationist person who works to protect something, such as a natural resource

crocodile thick-skinned reptile that lives in the water and has a thin and pointy snout. Many crocodiles live in Australia.

demonstration show or explain something. Irwin led popular animal demonstrations.

endangered in danger of dying out. American crocodiles were removed from the endangered species list in 2007.

exhibit display. A crocodile exhibit tells about the animals' diet, sleeping patterns, and habitat.

extinct died out. When a species is extinct, there are no more of that type of animal on Earth.

fauna animals. A fauna park is like a zoo.

global warming increase in the temperature of the Earth's atmosphere

habitat place in nature where an animal lives

herpetologist person who studies or takes care of reptiles

mammal furry, warm-blooded animal that feeds its young milk from its body. Humans are mammals.

naturalist person who studies nature

orphaned left without parents. The Irwins took in orphaned animals and cared for them.

poacher person who hunts illegally

predator animal that hunts and kills its prey. The crocodile is a deadly predator.

rare very few. Some rare species are in danger of dying out.

reptile scaly, cold-blooded animal that moves on its belly or on small, short legs. Crocodiles are a type of reptile.

stingray disk-shaped sea creature with a long, poisonous stinger. When a stingray is frightened, it may shoot up the sharp stinger (barb) on its tail.

volunteer someone who does something, such as work, for free. Many volunteers work to protect wildlife.

wombat small, furry animal with claws and sharp teeth

Want to Know More?

Books

Rau, Dana Meachen. *When Crocodiles Attack!* Berkeley Heights, NJ: Enslow, 2006.

Simon, Seymour. *Crocodiles and Alligators.* New York: HarperTrophy, 2001.

Wexo, John Bonnett. *Alligators and Crocodiles (Zoobooks).* Poway, CA.: Wildlife Education, 2003.

Websites

www.australiazoo.com
Read about Steve Irwin's life, his conservation projects, and about Australia Zoo animals.

www.bbc.co.uk/nature/reallywild/wildfile/wildfile_croc.shtml
Read about Nile crocodiles. See videos of adult crocodiles in the water and of crocodile eggs hatching.

www.nationalgeographic.com/ngkids/games/brainteaser/supercroc/supercroc.html
Visit National Geographic's Kid's Magazine to test your crocodile knowledge!

Places to visit

Australian Museum

6 College Street • Sydney • NSW 2010 • Australia (+612) 9320 6000
www.austmus.gov.au
This is Australia's oldest museum and its largest museum of natural history. It contains many exhibits on local animals, such as wombats, koalas, and crocodiles.

Australia Zoo
Steve Irwin Way • Beerwah • QLD 4519 • Australia (+617) 5436 2000
www.australiazoo.com
Home of the "Crocodile Hunter," this is the zoo founded by Steve Irwin's parents. Stop by to see wombats, tigers, cheetahs, lions, koalas, snakes, and, of course, lots of crocs!

INDEX